# SHARKS SET I

# HAMMERHEAD SHARKS

Heidi Mathea
ABDO Publishing Company

## visit us at
## www.abdopublishing.com

Printed in the United States of America, North Mankato, Minnesota.
042010
092010

 PRINTED ON RECYCLED PAPER

Cover Photo: Photolibrary
Interior Photos: Alamy p. 15; © Avi Klapfer/SeaPics.com p. 21; Copyright © Brandon Cole
    p. 17; © Doug Perrine/SeaPics.com pp. 6, 12; © D.R. Schrichte/SeaPics.com p. 11;
    © Jeremy Stafford-Deitsch/SeaPics.com pp. 18–19; © Masa Ushioda/SeaPics.com p. 10;
    Peter Arnold p. 8; © Rudie Kuiter/SeaPics.com p. 5; © Saul Gonor/SeaPics.com p. 19;
    © Stephen Kajiura/SeaPics.com p. 13; Uko Gorter pp. 7, 9

Editor: Megan M. Gunderson
Art Direction & Cover Design: Neil Klinepier

### Library of Congress Cataloging-in-Publication Data

Mathea, Heidi, 1979-
  Hammerhead sharks / Heidi Mathea.
      p. cm. -- (Sharks)
  Includes index.
  ISBN 978-1-61613-426-6
  1. Hammerhead sharks--Juvenile literature. I. Title.
  QL638.95.S7M38 2011
  597.3--dc22
                                        2010005542

# CONTENTS

# HAMMERHEADS AND FAMILY

Sharks are impressive fish.  They never fail to stir excitement or fear in people.  Unlike other fish, sharks do not have bones.  Instead, their skeletons are made of tough, stretchy tissue called cartilage.  This is much lighter than bone.  You have cartilage, too.  It is in your ears!

Rough, toothlike scales called denticles cover shark skin.  Denticles offer protection against predators.  They also help sharks easily move through water.

There are more than 400 living species of sharks.  Hammerhead sharks make up eight of these species.  They are named for their hammer-shaped heads.  These unusual shapes serve many purposes for these interesting creatures.

*Hammerhead sharks belong to the family Sphyrnidae.*

# WHAT THEY LOOK LIKE

The hammerhead's body is perfectly designed to move through its underwater world. The shark's fins and tail, or caudal fin, help it swim with ease.

The flattened head is called a cephalofoil. Its shape varies by species. For example, the great hammerhead has a rectangular head. The bonnethead has a head shaped like a shovel.

Size also varies among the species. The 3-foot (.9-m) scalloped bonnethead

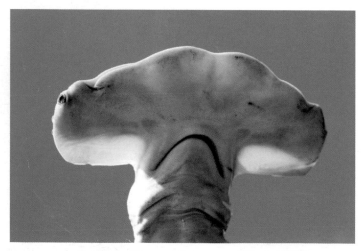

*A smalleye hammerhead's cephalofoil*

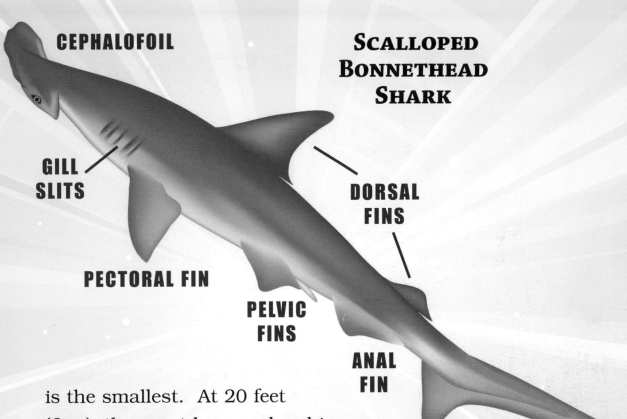

CEPHALOFOIL

SCALLOPED
BONNETHEAD
SHARK

GILL
SLITS

DORSAL
FINS

PECTORAL FIN

PELVIC
FINS

ANAL
FIN

CAUDAL FIN

is the smallest. At 20 feet (6 m), the great hammerhead is the largest.

All hammerheads are gray or brown along their backs and sides. The bellies are white. Each hammerhead has five pairs of gill slits along the sides of the head.

# WHERE THEY LIVE

Hammerhead sharks live in **temperate** and **tropical** oceans around the world. A hammerhead's **habitat** varies by species. In general, hammerheads swim in shallow coastal

**Scalloped hammerhead**

waters or above **continental shelves**. They may also be found far offshore.

Many hammerhead species swim alone, but some form schools. The bonnethead is often seen in groups of 3 to 15. The scalloped hammerhead is the only big hammerhead species known to form large schools.

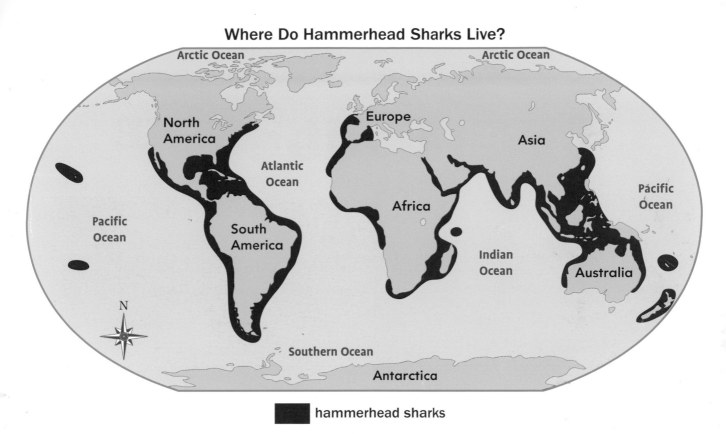

**Where Do Hammerhead Sharks Live?**

hammerhead sharks

Seasonally, some hammerhead shark species **migrate**. During the winter, they move toward the **equator** where the water is warmer. They travel toward the **poles** during the summer.

9

# FOOD

**Bonnethead sharks love to eat blue crabs.**

Most hammerheads feed in shallow water along coasts. They eat a variety of prey such as bony fish, squid, lobsters, and crabs. Larger hammerheads also feed on small sharks and bottom-dwelling fish.

Stingrays are a favorite meal for great hammerheads. In fact, these sharks are known to eat stingrays whole. This includes the poisonous tail spine!

*Great hammerheads are active hunters.*

Sharks don't usually eat as often as humans do. But when they do eat, they consume a lot! A shark may feast on a large meal every two or three days.

# SENSES

**Smalleye hammerhead**

    A hammerhead shark uses its oddly shaped head to its advantage.  A round eye is located on each end of the head.  This gives the shark a better range of vision than many other shark species.

The skin around a shark's head and the front end of its body is covered with sense **organs**. They sense the electric fields of living animals. The hammerhead shark's large head surface provides more area for these organs. This helps a hammerhead shark easily find prey.

Each hammerhead also finds prey using a lateral line system. The lateral lines are special organs located along a shark's

**Winghead shark**

body, just below the skin. They allow a shark to detect vibrations in the water. This can lead the shark to its next meal!

# BABIES

Hammerhead reproduction varies from species to species. Newborn hammerhead sharks are called pups. The number of pups a mother has ranges from 2 to 42. The smaller species produce fewer young than the larger species.

A female bonnethead is **pregnant** for five months. She gives birth to 4 to 14 pups. The pups are just over 12 inches (31 cm) long.

A great hammerhead mother carries her young for 11 months. She gives birth to 6 to 42 pups. The pups are about 24 inches (61 cm) long.

Pregnant hammerheads give birth to live pups in shallow, protected coastal waters. Then, the mothers swim away. Left on their own, the pups use their well-developed senses to survive.

Scalloped hammerhead pups

# ATTACK AND DEFENSE

Hammerhead sharks are skilled hunters. They have many rows of teeth to catch prey. There are several rows of new teeth below the working teeth. When a tooth is lost or damaged, a new one replaces it.

The teeth of smaller hammerhead species such as bonnetheads are thick and flattened. These teeth are suited to crushing the shellfish they prey on.

Larger hammerheads have huge, bladelike teeth. A bigger hammerhead also uses its head to attack prey. Using its large cephalofoil, the shark rams and pins prey.

Hammerhead sharks can also become prey. Smaller hammerheads rely on their senses to avoid large bony fish and other sharks. Large, adult hammerheads have almost nothing to fear except man. Humans hunt hammerheads for food and products such as vitamins and leather.

**The great hammerhead shark is fished for its highly valued fins.**

# ATTACKS ON HUMANS

Most hammerhead sharks are not dangerous to humans. However, great and smooth hammerheads are **aggressive**. These large sharks are considered dangerous to man. Hammerheads are responsible for 21 **unprovoked** attacks on humans.

Follow a few rules to avoid encountering a shark. Don't swim alone. Stay near shore and away from areas where fishing occurs. Sharks are attracted to the blood of injured fish.

Sharks may attack humans, but they are not hunting them. The sharks may just be curious. Humans should respect sharks when they see them in the water.

Great hammerhead
sharks can be curious
about divers.

Smooth hammerheads prefer cooler water.
So, they rarely encounter humans.

# HAMMERHEAD SHARK FACTS

**Scientific Name:**

| | |
|---|---|
| Bonnethead | *Sphyrna tiburo* |
| Great hammerhead | *Sphyrna mokarran* |
| Scalloped bonnethead | *Sphyrna corona* |
| Scalloped hammerhead | *Sphyrna lewini* |
| Scoophead | *Sphyrna media* |
| Smalleye hammerhead | *Sphyrna tudes* |
| Smooth hammerhead | *Sphyrna zygaena* |
| Winghead shark | *Eusphyra blochii* |

**Average Size:**

Hammerheads are 3 to 20 feet (.9 to 6 m) long.

**Where They're Found:**

Hammerheads live worldwide in temperate and tropical seas.

Schooling scalloped hammerheads

# GLOSSARY

**aggressive** (uh-GREH-sihv) - displaying hostility.

**continental shelf** - a shallow, underwater plain forming a continent's border. It ends with a steep slope to the deep ocean floor.

**equator** - an imaginary circle around the middle of Earth. It is halfway between the North and South poles.

**habitat** - a place where a living thing is naturally found.

**migrate** - to move from one place to another, often to find food.

**organ** - a part of an animal or a plant composed of several kinds of tissues. An organ performs a specific function. The heart, liver, gallbladder, and intestines are organs of an animal.

**pole** - either end of Earth's axis. The North Pole and the South Pole are opposite each other.

**pregnant** - having one or more babies growing within the body.

**temperate** - relating to an area where average temperatures range between 50 and 55 degrees Fahrenheit (10 and 13°C).

**tropical** - relating to an area with an average temperature above 77 degrees Fahrenheit (25°C) where no freezing occurs.

**unprovoked** - not prompted to action by anything done or said.

# WEB SITES

To learn more about hammerhead sharks, visit ABDO Publishing Company on the World Wide Web at **www.abdopublishing.com**. Web sites about hammerhead sharks are featured on our Book Links page. These links are routinely monitored and updated to provide the most current information available.

# INDEX